fantastic
gel candles

fantastic
gel candles

35 Fun &
Creative
Projects

Marcianne Miller

LARK BOOKS
A Division of Sterling Publishing Co., Inc.
New York

Art Director: CELIA NARANJO
Photography: EVAN BRACKEN
Cover Design: BARBARA ZARETSKY
Production Assistance: HANNES CHAREN, THERESA GWYNN
Editorial Assistance: THERESA GWYNN, RAIN NEWCOMB

Library of Congress Cataloging-in-Publication Data

Miller, Marcianne.
    Fantastic gel candles : 35 fun & creative projects / by Marcianne Miller.
       p. cm.
    Includes index.
    ISBN 1-57990-283-9 (pbk.)
    1. Candlemaking. I. Title.

TT896.5 .M55 2002
745.593'32—dc21   2001038050

10 9 8 7 6 5 4 3 2 1

First Edition

Published by Lark Books, a division of
Sterling Publishing Co., Inc.
387 Park Avenue South, New York, N.Y. 10016

© 2002, Lark Books

Distributed in Canada by Sterling Publishing,
c/o Canadian Manda Group, One Atlantic Ave., Suite 105
Toronto, Ontario, Canada M6K 3E7

Distributed in the U.K. by:
Guild of Master Craftsman Publications Ltd.
Castle Place, 166 High Street, Lewes East Sussex, England BN7 1XU
Tel: (+ 44) 1273 477374, Fax: (+ 44) 1273 478606,
Email: pubs@thegmcgroup.com, Web: www.gmcpublications.com

Distributed in Australia by Capricorn Link (Australia) Pty Ltd., P.O. Box 704, Windsor, NSW 2756 Australia.

If you have questions or comments about this book, please contact:
Lark Books
67 Broadway
Asheville, NC 28801
(828) 236-9730

Printed in Hong Kong
ISBN 1-57990-283-9

This book is dedicated to Barney Chester, whose flame will never fade.

Contents

Gel Candlemaking Basics

Beautiful, easy to create, affordable, fun for families to make together, and lovely to give away as gifts—it's no wonder gel candles have become phenomenally popular! In *Fantastic Gel Candles*, you'll find information to help you jump easily from novice gel candlemaker to master. You'll learn the nature of gel and which creative techniques and safety tips work with it; how to choose containers and embeds that bring out the beauty of the gel; how to cause or prevent bubbles, create special effects, and recycle gel—and how to personalize your gel candles so they always display your unique touch.

There are four key elements to a successful gel candle: the gel itself and what you can do to it; the containers that hold the gel; the embeds and other objects you put into the gel; and the wick that transforms the combination of the other elements into a candle you can light and enjoy.

All About Gel

Gel candle wax is a specialized mineral oil (a by-product of the distillation of petroleum) that has been mixed with a chemical agent to thicken it to a gelatin-like consistency.

Gel is no more dangerous than the oil you rub on a baby's skin. Of course, you shouldn't eat gel (you don't eat baby oil, do you?), but if you did accidentally swallow some, it wouldn't kill you. The oil is not digestible; it would just go right through your system.

Knowing that the gel is oil tells you other things. If you get gel on a silk shirt, it will probably leave a permanent stain. But most porous materials that come into contact with the gel—work clothes, dishtowels, and tablecloths, for example—can be laundered safely with a grease-eating detergent.

No other candles compare with the translucent beauty of gel candles.

Gel candlemaking requires only a few basic materials and equipment.

Removing gel from nonporous surfaces is easy once you learn the secret—wait until the gel has cooled. If you try to wipe gel spills from glass containers when the gel is hot, for example, you'll just smear the gel and make a bigger cleanup chore. You can peel off cooled gel easily. Ammonia, adhesive-tape removers, mineral spirits, and other grease-cutting cleansers work best.

Big globs of spilled gel are better than little globs. You can see big globs of gel, after all. But little globs—oh dear!—they can get in, on, under, and around just about anything! Although you don't have to be a precision-nut in most aspects of gel candlemaking, it does help to be very neat and careful with the gel so you don't drive yourself crazy trying to clean up later.

Keep the gel—even tiny bits of it—off your stove-top burners. Gel on burners is hard to see, but you'll know it's there the next time you use the burner and the stinky burned gel sets off your smoke alarm! As you pour gel, it can run down the sides of the pan, and end up on the burner when you return the pan to the stove. To help you avoid gel spills, we recommend using certain types of pans and utensils. (See Gel Candlemaking Tools, page 11.)

Gel is wonderfully recyclable. Don't like the way a candle turned out? Just re-melt the gel and try again. Tired of the royal blue candles you made for the holidays? Re-melt the gel, add some green dye, and create a beautiful, sea-goddess-green candle to inspire dreams of summer at the beach. Fun, huh?

Gel oil should never go down the drain. If you want to discard it, do the same thing you would with bacon grease—let it solidify in a covered metal container, and throw it out it with your trash.

MAKING GEL CANDLES—SAFETY FIRST

Because gel is made with oil, it's flammable—that's why it's used to make candles. Unless you're using beeswax or coconut oil-based candles, most of the candles you've burned in your life—paraffin wax candles—are also refined from petroleum.

Oil and water don't mix, so if you should overheat the gel and it catches fire—water won't put the fire out. Think of a gel fire as a grease fire and you'll already know how to handle it—smother the fire with a pan lid to starve it of oxygen. Keep a big lid set out and ready to use—you don't want to have to scramble for it in a panic. You can also smother a small fire with baking soda—which now comes in a shaker-top container that is much easier to handle in a hurry than opening up the old-fashioned box. Of course, you should have a fire extinguisher in the kitchen at all times. Know how to use it and keep it within easy reach.

Liquid gel is hot enough to melt a plastic ladle, but not hot enough to ignite newspaper if you dropped hot gel on it. But if you spill liquid gel on yourself, it *will* hurt! Hot gel will stick to your skin and hold its high temperature on *you* long enough to cause a significant burn. In other words, be careful! And use those kitchen mitts and potholders. If you should suffer a hot gel burn, treat the burned area immediately by applying ice, and follow up with medical care, if necessary.

Your gel candlemaking work area should be well-ventilated, well-lit, and efficiently laid out so you don't have to fumble for knives, skewers, and other sharp utensils.

If you're new to gel candlemaking, you'll be amazed by how quickly the gel liquefies. Don't try to speed up an already speedy process by turning up the heat—the gel can reach its flash point more quickly than you expect. And don't even think about

Center your gel-heating pan in the middle of the burner. Position the handle to face the back of the stove, where you won't bump into it.

heating gel in the microwave. It doesn't work, it may injure you, and it will ruin your microwave.

You might think that large batches of gel will melt quickly too, but the truth is it can take a surprisingly long time to melt large batches. Be patient! You can speed things up—safely—if you crumble the gel into small pieces with your hands before putting it into the pan. Especially when you work with large batches of gel, wear protective eyewear to prevent injury from hot gel splatters.

When you're heating gel, stay with the gel. Never leave it unattended. No matter how multi-tasked you may be in the rest of your life, you can not be in two places at one time when heating gel.

Standard kitchen fire safety equipment—and common sense—ensure safe gel candlemaking.

Respect gel's potential for danger—and you'll be safe.

BURNING GEL CANDLES—SAFETY FIRST

Many people prefer candles made from gel because they burn so long—at least twice as long as candles made from paraffin. An 8-ounce (.2 L) gel candle (about the size of a coffee mug) can burn for 100 hours or longer!

Children, Dogs, Cats, and Other Beloved Dangers

Most gel candlemakers are women, and many enjoy making crafts with their families. Gel candlemaking is a wonderful activity for adults and older children to do together. However—gel candles and young children do not mix!

Young children should not be present when you're making gel candles. They can hurt themselves on the hot gel, or distract you, which could result in an injury to either one, or both of you. Gel candles are especially attractive to young children, who are fascinated by the gel's transparency and 3-D effects. Youngsters may eagerly reach for gel candles, unmindful of the possible dangers. Our policy is simple: Keep gel candles away from *young* children.

And, unless you want cat paw prints in your gel cutouts, and dog hair in your gel party roses— not to mention the possibility of being tripped while carrying a pan of hot gel—keep *all* furry folks out of your working area.

Gel candles also burn hotter than paraffin candles. Gel candles have pool temperatures (the pool is the circle of melted gel around the wick) ranging from 245°F to 280°F (118°C to 137°C)—compared to paraffin wax pool temperatures of 180°F (82°C) or higher.

Although they burn longer and hotter, gel candles have smaller flames, which means it's easy to forget you've got a gel candle burning. Not a good idea!! If a gel candle is allowed to burn for too long, it can get *very* hot, and may burst into a flame so big you don't even want to think about how dangerous it could be!

If you make gel candles as gifts (and what gel candlemaker doesn't?), it would be an excellent idea to print the safety tips on a card and include it with your candles. (See How to Burn Your Gel Candle Safely on the next page. You have our permission to reproduce these tips.)

WHERE TO FIND GEL

Gel comes in different grades. The medium polymer (MP) grade is the most popular among candlemakers and is the one we used in the projects in the book. Craft stores usually sell MP candle gel wax in solid form in small tubs. You can order larger amounts through the stores or contact the distributors directly. In North America, most distributors of gel wax and accessories have toll-free telephone numbers, and many have Web sites on the Internet, where you can place orders and keep up with the latest news in gel candlemaking. Just type in "gel candles" on your search engine; you'll find an amazing number of resources, including newsletters for virtual neighborhoods of gel candlemakers!

HOW MUCH GEL?

Pour water into your candle container until the water reaches the level that you'd like the gel to reach. Then measure the water by pouring it into a measuring cup—that's the amount of liquefied gel you'll need. After the first few times of measuring precisely, you'll get pretty good at eyeballing how much gel you need.

GETTING STARTED

There are two ways to get the gel out of the container. Do your Miss Manners imitation and try to remove it with a large spoon—but it's not easy to push the spoon through the hard gel, and you may end up in a most unladylike snit! Or dig right into it with your bare hands—hey, gel candlemaking is supposed to bring out the creative child in you! Once you get out those first few clumps with your hands, the rest of the gel will come out easily with a spoon. In no time at all, you'll get used to gel's rubbery texture.

GEL CANDLEMAKING TOOLS

Those who make paraffin candles may wonder why gel candlemakers don't use double boilers to liquefy the gel. The reason is simple: You can't achieve temperatures in a double boiler that are high enough to liquefy gel. An ordinary *stove-top saucepan* that is light enough for you to handle is fine for heating the solid gel. The ideal pan has two features: a *pour spout* on the rim that makes it easy to pour the gel into the containers without spilling the gel, and a heat-resistant handle. Just scrub the pan well with a grease-dissolving dish detergent after each use.

A *clip-on pan thermometer* is essential—using it is the only way to measure the gel temperature accurately.

How to Burn Your Gel Candle Safely

- Don't leave a burning candle unattended.
- Don't burn gel candles for longer than 2 hours at any one time.
- Don't burn the candle all the way down to bottom of the container. Leave at least 1 inch (2.5 cm) of gel in the bottom.
- Keep the wicks short! The longer the wick, the higher and hotter the flame—and the more likely the gel is to ignite.
- The first time you burn a candle, the wick should be $1/4$ inch (6 mm) high.
- Every time you light a candle after the first time, trim the wick to $1/6$ inch (1.5 mm). That's right—*really* short!!
- Place candles on flat, nonporous, heat-resistant surfaces.
- Keep candles out of the reach of children and pets. If you suspect a child has eaten a gel candle, call your Poison Control Center immediately.

You don't want to make the beginner's foolish mistake—testing the temperature of the hot gel by sticking your finger into it!

Even better than the pan-and-thermometer combination is an *electric slow cooker with an adjustable temperature control*. This handy appliance can be set to a specific temperature and will maintain it, making the process of liquefying the gel safe and easy.

The small tools for gel candlemaking are inexpensive and easy to find.

Ladles help you control the pour of the gel. We recommend two—a large one and a small one—for containers of different sizes and for a variety of pouring jobs.

Metal spoons and *metal skewers* are the only ones you should use when stirring gel or inserting embeds. Don't use wood utensils; wood can react chemically with the gel and cause it to bubble excessively.

Cookie sheets are extremely handy. Use them to help you safely carry candles to the oven for slow cooling or reheating, and to make large sheets of colored gel.

A *pizza cutter*, which has a circular, rotating blade, is an excellent tool for slicing layers of gel. In fact, we found that it was the only tool that did the job easily.

A *bubble stick* is a long flat plastic stirrer that helps reduce the number of bubbles after you've poured the gel into the container. You can find bubble sticks in stores that sell food-canning supplies.

Utility knives, hot-glue guns, tweezers, pliers, wire cutters, scissors, a tape measure, and felt-tip markers—as you make gel candles, you'll probably use one or more of these tools at one time or another.

Gathering all your tools and reserving them just for candlemaking—including several pans—is more efficient in the long run; you won't have to interrupt your creative urges by rummaging through the junk drawer looking for that tool you must have *now*.

HEATING GEL

Although the term "melt" is commonly used among gel candlemakers, the truth is gel doesn't really melt. It simply decreases in viscosity—or liquefies—as it is heated. Conversely, as the liquid gel is cooled, it increases in viscosity—or solidifies to its hardened, gel, state. Unlike paraffin, which has a definite point at which it melts, gel's liquefy/solidify process takes place gradually, over a range of temperatures.

Heating gel is a process of achieving the right temperature range for what you want the gel to do. For example, you must first heat gel at a high enough temperature to liquefy it. But if you add items such as dye or fragrance—which require time to stir thoroughly—the gel loses some heat. So you may need to re-heat the gel. Depending on how much gel you are heating, what you put into it, and how high you want the pouring temperature to be (which relates to how many bubbles you want), the time it takes to reach a temperature range can take anywhere from a few seconds to many minutes.

Gels produced by different manufacturers can vary. That's why, in all the instructions for the projects in this book, we refer you to the manufacturer's recommendations, which are included on the gel package, or available from the manufacturer.

On the other hand, we realize that, for any number of unforeseen reasons, a very small minority of our readers might not have the manufacturer's recommendations. Rather than having a reader guess —and guess *wrong*—about gel's temperature ranges, we offer the following ranges of temperatures as guidelines to help if you're in a pinch. Be aware that temperatures in your particular candlemaking situation can vary considerably from these ranges.

- The "melting" or liquefying range, when solid gel becomes liquid (the consistency of corn syrup) is 180°F to 220°F (82°C to 104°C).
- The pouring range is 190°F to 205°F (88°C to 96°C).
  - If you want a lot of bubbles, pour at a temperature at the lower end of the range.
  - If you want fewer bubbles, pour at a temperature at the higher end of the range.
- The baking or reheating range is 170°F to 175°F (77°C to 79°C).
- The cooling range, when the liquid gel becomes solid, is 140°F to 167°F (60°C to 75°C).

Warning: Never heat gel as high as 230°F (110°C). It's unsafe—gel can start burning at this temperature. And it's wasteful—if you scorch the gel, it's ruined and there's no way to save it. You'll have to discard it.

Remember—you can't tell what the temperature of gel is just by looking at it. Always use a clip-on thermometer—or the adjustable temperature control on the electric slow cooker—to ensure the safe and beautiful production of your gel candles.

Some candlemakers experiment with different temperature ranges to suit their specific situations—but what works for them may not work for you. Our advice is to stay on the side of extreme caution, following manufacturer's recommendations and your good common sense.

CONQUERING BUBBLES

Gel candlemakers tend to fall into two camps: Bubble Haters and Bubble Lovers. We admit we are tiptoe-ing toward the Bubble-Lover camp. After all, bubbles are a part of gel, and these are gel candles we're making. And even if we didn't like bubbles, we know that, no matter what we do, sometimes bub-bles appear!

The six causes of bubbles are: 1) the temperature of the container; 2) the temperature of the gel when you pour it; 3) the pouring method you use; 4) the reaction of the gel to items you put into it, such as spoons, fragrances and embeds; 5) the method you use to cool the gel; and 6) who knows?

How successfully you deal with these causes depends on your experience, skill—and luck!

Preheat Your Container

Warm up your container before you pour the gel into it by putting the container in a 175°F (80°C) oven for about 10 minutes. After a while, it's easy to remember to do this. Just put the container in the oven right after you put the gel in the pan or slow cooker. (It's easy to forget an empty container is hot. Remember to use protection on your hands when you remove the empty container from the oven.)

Check Your Pouring Temperature

Generally, the higher the pouring temperature, the fewer the bubbles. That means for *each* candle. When you're making more than one candle at a time, dou-ble check the temperature before you pour each candle. Melted gel cools quickly. You might have a temperature at the high end of the pouring range when you pour your first candle, but in just a few minutes between pours, the gel temperature could drop low enough to produce twice as many bubbles in the later candles.

Perfect Your Pouring Method

The way you pour the gel affects how much air gets into it, thus affecting how many bubbles will form. To minimize bubbles, pour the gel as you would pour a beer to get less suds—by holding the container at an angle and pouring slowly.

Add Only Bubble-Friendly Items

Anything you put into the gel should be compatible with it. Fragrances and embeds that are not compati-ble with gel, for example, cause excessive bubbling. See the section on Fragrances, page 18. Also see the section on Embeds, page 20, which goes into detail about what kinds of embeds are compatible.

Even the perfect embed will cause bubbles if it has impurities, including water, on it. Wash and dry thor-oughly any object that you want to embed.

Pretreat embeds to test them and give them a pro-tective seal. Pour a small amount of hot gel into a bowl, and coat the items in the gel. Watch for bub-bles. If none appear, use tweezers to remove the items, holding them over the gel to let the excess gel drip back into the bowl. If bubbles do appear, stir occasionally, leaving the embeds in the gel until the bubbling stops. If, after a few minutes, the bubbling continues, either decide not to use those embeds, or

Glass bulbs on wire are gel compatible embeds.

live with the bubbles. Don't make candles with the gel that you've used to pretreat ebeds.

Right after you pour the gel, if you gently stir it with a bubble stick, you can decrease the bubbling. If bubbles appear on the surface, just prick them with a pin.

Experiment with Gel Cooling Methods

Bubble Conquerors are divided into two opposing camps: the Fast Coolers and the Slow Coolers. On the theory that quick cooling arrests the formation of bubbles, the Fast Coolers place their gel candles into the refrigerator immediately after pouring. (Rest the candle on a bed of dishtowels or other heat resistant cushion so the hot container doesn't break a cold glass refrigerator shelf.)

The Slow Coolers attempt to decrease bubbles by slow cooling, such as leaving the candles undisturbed in a secure place—even outdoors on a sunny day—

for several hours. You can actively slow down the cooling process by wrapping the candles in towels or baking them in a warm (175°F or 80°C) oven for several hours, even overnight.

Which method works? They all do. Since each candlemaker's environment, technique, additives, equipment, and patience level differs, our advice is to experiment with both fast and slow methods of cooling and find out what works best for you. A notebook with a record of your findings can be invaluable.

Re-Heat Some Candles

If a candle develops bubbles (it's amazing how they do reappear!), you can reheat many kinds of gel candles in the oven. Usually, but *not* always, the reheating process will reduce the bubbling. Remember the obvious, though: you can't reheat layered candles (the layers will melt into one another), or candles with floating embeds (the embeds will sink), or candles with meltable embeds, such as wax embeds.

When you want to reheat a candle, place it on a cookie sheet before setting it in the oven. In a worst-case scenario, the candle container might shatter and the gel spill. Make sure the oven rack is level so your gel surface doesn't harden lopsided.

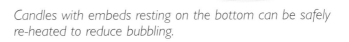

Candles with embeds resting on the bottom can be safely re-heated to reduce bubbling.

ENHANCING GEL WITH COLOR

You can create fantastic candles by playing with gel's capacity to accept color easily. The techniques are simple, fun to learn, and forgiving—if you don't like the results, you can liquefy the gel and start over. In *Fantastic Gel Candles*, we played with color in four basic ways: by tinting the whole candle, making layers of different colors, making appliqués, and making molds.

Using Dye

There are excellent dyes made specifically for gel candles and you can also use dyes made for traditional paraffin candles. You can't use food coloring—it's water-soluble and doesn't mix with oil.

Dye comes in two forms—liquid and solid—and a little bit of either goes a long way. To color gel, heat the gel until it's completely liquefied (see Heating Gel, page 13), then gently stir in small amounts of dye, with a metal spoon, until you have the color you want. With liquid dyes, add a few drops at a time. For solid dyes, use a food grater to scrape the dye into small pieces.

Keep a handful of small gel candle containers near your work area. If you end up with too much dyed gel, just pour it into the stand-bys (Lots of Little Squares, page 24). Or remove hardened gel from the pan and store it in a sealable plastic bag or a glass container with a lid.

Testing the Color

Dyed gel looks darker in the pan than it will in the candle, so test the color before pouring. Place a small amount of the tinted gel in a glass or place a few drops on a sheet of heavy, white paper.

Allow the gel to solidify, and then see how you like the color. If the color appears too dark, simply dilute it by adding more clear gel to the pan. If the color appears too light, just add more dye.

Making Layers of Color

Making candles with different colored layers of gel is as easy as dying gel for an entire candle—it just takes longer to make more colors. Successful layering depends on your choice of colors and how you arrange them. Use your own good color sense to guide you. Red and green, for example, will eventually blend into a muddy brown color where the layers meet, but red and blue will blend to form a nice purplish color.

Layers in gel candles tend to be less distinct because the transparent nature of the gel seems to blend the colors. To create layers that are as distinct as possible, allow each layer to cool and harden completely before you pour the next layer.

Be patient. A candle with several layers can take many hours to complete. See the techniques for horizontal layering in Tower of Pizzazz, page 76, and the angled layering in Tri-Color Garden Torches, page 90.

Making Appliqués of Color

Experienced gel candlemakers have learned the wisdom of preparing sheets of gel ahead of time, so that

they're handy when the inspiration for a new gel appliqué candle hits them. Line a cookie sheet with aluminum foil, placing the shiny side of the foil face up. (The shiny side is smoother, so the gel won't stick to it.) Spray any cooking oil—or lubricating oil, such as the oil you use to fix a squeaky door—onto the foil.

Pour dyed gel onto the foil-covered cookie sheet to make layers. For thin appliqués for small candles (Fairy Flower Pots, page 75), make $1/6$ to $1/8$-inch-thick (1.6 mm to 3 mm) layers. For thicker appliqués (Polka Dot Delight, page 80), and strips of gel (Sensational Sushi, page 86), make each layer $1/4$ inch (6mm) thick. When the gel is cool, cut out shapes with cookie cutters; use a pizza cutter to slice out strips of gel.

If you don't need a whole cookie sheet of gel, make smaller "trays" of foil on the cookie sheet: cut a dou-

bled layer of foil to the size tray you want, fold up the sides, and fold and pinch the corners together.

To keep dyed gel sheets for future use, cut them into convenient sizes and place them between pieces of waxed paper. Put the wrapped gel into sealable bags or containers, and store them in the refrigerator.

Making Molds

Using muffin tins or soapmaking molds to create gel candles easily expands your candlemaking possibilities. Just dye the gel, pour it into the mold, and let it cool. Because they're tiny, small gel mold candles are more for show than for practical use; they melt quickly once their wicks are lit. (But oh, how impressive they are while they last!)

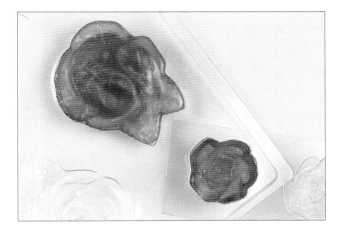

If you use plastic molds as we did in Pink Party Roses (page 92), pour the gel at the lower temperature range to avoid melting the mold. The key to success with molds is twofold. First, the mold needs to rest flat. Fill the mold with water. If the water fills the mold completely, the mold is flat. If the mold isn't flat, make it so by securely propping the mold up with towels or scrap aluminum foil. Secondly, use a ladle to control pouring the gel into the small molds.

ENHANCING GEL WITH FRAGRANCE

Fragrances add a delightful, second sensory pleasure to the visual beauty of gel candles. Many—but not all—of the fragrances used in paraffin candles can also be used in gel candles. Fragrances can contain chemicals—sometimes, as many as 50 different aroma chemicals can go into the composition of a fragrance. When chemicals mix, they don't always react positively with one another.

That's what can happen with gel and fragrances that aren't compatible. And that's why the addition of fragrances to gel is a major safety issue for candlemakers.

A compatible fragrance is often referred to as *non-polar*, which means that it is compatible with the hydrocarbons that make up the mineral oil gel. When you see the term non-polar on the label of a candle fragrance, you know that fragrance is fine for use in gel candles.

Fragrances have two areas of compatibility with gel—solubility and flash point.

Solubility refers to the ability of the fragrance to dissolve easily in the gel. A compatible fragrance is oil-soluble and melds beautifully with the gel and becomes invisible. But an incompatible fragrance can cloud the gel.

Flash point refers to the temperature at which a substance will burst into flame. Most fragrances have a flash point of 140°F (60°C). The preferred flash point for fragrances in gel candles however is no lower than 170°F (77°C), which means that adding fragrance to gel can cause a candle's flash point to go lower—and the gel can burst into flame at a lower temperature than it would without the fragrance. Thus, there has been—and still is—concern about the safe use of fragrances in gel candles.

Our advice is to use a fragrance only if you know it's compatible with the gel. The easiest way to be sure is to buy fragrances with labels that indicate they are gel compatible. If there's no label on the fragrance, here's a test to determine if it's compatible. Mix one part fragrance with three parts mineral oil. If the fragrance mixes in completely, with no cloudiness, it's fine for gel. If it separates out or makes the oil cloudy, don't use it in your gel candles. Don't use perfume. It contains alcohol and won't mix well with the oil-based gel.

Adding scents requires a delicate touch. Experts suggest that the fragrance load for the MP grade of gel (the one that is most commonly used) should be only 3 to 5 percent. Add the scent just before you pour the gel into the container so that the heat doesn't evaporate it immediately. Mix the fragrance gently but thoroughly into the gel. If the fragrance is not mixed throughout, it can cause the flame to burn unevenly or make the gel cloudy.

ENHANCING GEL WITH GLITTER

Gel glitter is a finely grained, gel-compatible additive that gives a lovely sheen to gel. Follow the manufacturer's directions on the package. Add the glitter to the gel after you've added the dye and just before pouring. As with fragrance, a little bit of glitter goes a long way, so experiment with a light touch first.

All About Containers

Unlike traditional candles, in which the container is just something that holds the candles, gel candle containers share equal billing with the gel. Often, it's the container itself that inspires a candle. Containers range from practical and homey to sophisticated and spectacular—with a lot of creative space in between.

In general, choose glassware that is designed to be stable so it won't tip over easily. Thick glass containers are sturdy, and because they slow down the cooling process, often help prevent bubbling. Very thin glass may not handle the heat of the gel. For proper heat dissemination, the top of a gel candle container should not be narrower than the bottom, and the top should be at least 2 to 3 inches (5 to 7.6 cm) wide.

Glass is the preferred material for gel candle containers because it shows off the gel's beauty, but you can also use porcelain and pottery containers (Candy Dish Surprises, page 47).

EVERYDAY GLASS

Start your search for gel candle containers in your own home. Drinking glasses, glass mugs, orphaned or outdated goblets, and vases that no longer hold their appeal make wonderful gel candle containers. Colored glass containers are great for timid beginners—just add the gel and the wick, and get the applause! Empty

glass food jars are excellent containers, especially if they have lids, which give the candles a finished look when they're not in use, and which also make it easy and safe to pack the candles for shipping.

DECORATED CONTAINERS

Glass containers come in two basic categories: glass that is already decorated beautifully in itself, such as etched glass, glass with decals, and pressed glass; or glass that is quite ordinary until the gel candlemaker transforms it (Simply Sequins, page 30). For many gel candlemakers, creating beautiful containers, especially painting or decorating glass, is as important as mastering the techniques of working with the gel.

COLLECTIBLE GLASS

Many of us have vintage glass that's been handed down through the family but doesn't suit our contemporary decorating style. When you take those old glasses out of hiding and turn them into gel candles, they look terrific in any décor (Vintage Charmers, page 26).

SHOW-OFF CONTAINERS

Deep, wide bowls are ideal when an expanse of clear gel is a key element in your design (Zen Rock Garden, page 48), or when you have lots of pretty objects (Sunken Treasure, page 62).

Tall cylinders make spectacular gel candles (Tower of Pizzazz, page 76). Reality check: Most of the gel in tall candles never gets burned because you can't reach down far enough inside to cut the wick. If you love tall candles the way we do— just for the pure pleasure of looking at them—go for it. Gel burns so slowly that you'll get many hours of enjoyment, no matter how much of the gel you eventually melt and reuse. Remember that in a narrow candle, the hottest part of the candle—the pool around the wick—has no space to spread and dissipate the heat. Two things could happen. The high heat could shatter the glass. Or the gel could get so hot it could ignite. Our advice: avoid very narrow containers.

All About Embeds

Embeds are the objects placed into the gel that can be seen through the glass container. For some gel candlemakers, finding and placing embeds is their favorite part of the craft. Embeds are everywhere—in drawers of old jewelry, children's toy boxes, antique shop bargain bins—anywhere small treasures are kept.

Besides deciding how attractive an embed will be in a candle, you'll have three other considerations: safety, gel compatibility, and placement of the embed in the candle.

SAFETY AND COMPATIBILITY CONCERNS

The safety of an embed in a gel candle relates to its flammability. There are non-flammable embeds, meltable embeds, and flammable embeds.

Non-Flammable Embeds:

The good news is most non-flammable embeds are also compatible with gel, meaning they are less likely to cause cloudiness or excessive bubbling.

Glass embeds accentuate gel's 3-D effect, especially when several are used in the same candle and placed at various levels.

Ceramic and pottery embeds come in a variety of shapes and sizes. Even broken pieces of pottery can look terrific in a candle.

Metal embeds are wonderful in gel candles, particularly since metal can range from thin wire shapes to solid forms such as coins and bells.

Natural ingredients, such as rocks, pebbles, and seashells, are both sturdy and elegant in candles.

Meltable Embeds

You can mold paraffin wax embeds yourself or purchase them readymade at craft stores or on the Internet. The trick with wax embeds is to avoid melting them with hot gel. Just heat the gel to the point where it's pourable but not completely liquid. Pour at least 1 inch (2.5 cm) of this gel over the embed, which will seal it. Fill the rest of the container with hotter gel.

Flammable Embeds

Objects such as photographs, paper, wood items, silk flowers, and fabric swatches should not be used as embeds. Even though you may not think of plastic and rubber as flammable, they certainly are at high temperatures, and they should not be used either. There are so many wonderful—and safe—things to use as embeds, why risk using materials that aren't safe or about which you have doubts? If you don't know whether an item is flammable or not, don't use it as a gel candle embed. If you insist on using it, then keep it at least 1 inch (2.5 cm) away from the wick.

PLACING EMBEDS

Tweezers and metal cooking skewers are helpful tools when you're working with embeds. Use them to place embeds in the container before you pour the gel and to reposition them, if necessary, after the gel has been poured.

If you want to position your embeds at specific heights in the container, suspend them with sewing thread that's tied to a skewer placed across the rim of the container, before you pour the gel. This is what

Use tweezers to place embeds, like these costume jewelry pieces, into gel.

we did in Gold Angels in a Goblet (page 38). If your embed doesn't have a hook or hole for the thread, then use two or three lengths of thread to create a "hammock," and hang them that way. After the gel has been poured and has cooled, gently tug on the threads to remove them.

All About Wicks

Wicks are the unsung heroines of gel candles. Their type, size, preparation, positioning, and maintenance are crucial to both the appearance and safety of gel candles.

SELECT THE PROPER WICK TYPE

Zinc-cored wicks are stiff and thus stay straight when they're inserted into the gel; they're the wicks of choice for most gel candlemakers. These wicks come in several styles—with or without anchor tabs and with or without waxing. An anchor tab is a good safety feature because it helps prevent the wick from burning to the very bottom of the candle. Do not use cotton or paper-cored wicks.

SELECT THE PROPER WICK SIZE

Wicks come in an assortment of sizes. Select a size that's appropriate for the size of your container. Refer to the wick manufacturer's instructions for guidance, but this is a general rule of thumb for zinc-cored wicks: small for containers with diameters of 2 to 3 inches (5.1 to 7.6 cm), medium for 3 to 4 inches (7.6 to 10.2 cm), and large for 4 to 5 inches (10.2 to 12.7 cm).

You can burn a candle only as far down as you can trim the wick—so there's no point in using a wick that goes all the way down to the bottom of the candle, unless the container is wide enough to allow you to reach in and trim the wick. A short wick is fine in a tall candle, especially a tall *narrow* candle.

Don't be tempted to use a wider wick just because gel candles burn twice as slowly as paraffin candles. A wick that is too wide can cause the flame to burn too hot—and ignite the gel.

PREPARE THE WICK FOR GEL

To reduce bubbling, pretreat your wicks, especially wax-coated wicks. Coat the wicks in hot melted gel and leave them in the gel until the bubbling stops. Remove the wicks, wait at least 30 seconds, and then run your fingers down them to remove the excess gel.

POSITION THE WICK PROPERLY

Attach an anchor wick to the bottom of the container before you pour the gel. Dip the end of the wick into hot gel and press it against the bottom of the container with a metal skewer. Or use a hot-glue gun to fasten it to the bottom. (The glue may react with the gel and cause some bubbling but the wick will be very secure.)

It's easy to keep wicks straight. Wrap the end of the wick around a skewer positioned on top of the container. When the gel is almost cool, tug the wick to make it taut.

Loop the other end of the wick around a skewer or pencil and position it over the top of the container. After you pour the gel and it is almost cool, give the wick a gentle tug to remove any slack. When the gel is cool, remove the wick from the skewer or pencil and trim it to ¼ inch (6 mm). Save the rest of the wick to use as short wicks for other candles.

Another way to insert a wick is to pour the gel first, and when the gel is almost cool, insert the wick from the top. If you want the wick to go into the gel more than a few inches, first insert a length of thin, sturdy wire through the gel to make a narrow hole. Remove the wire and, using the tunnel it left in the gel as a guide, insert the wick, keeping it at least 1 inch (2.5 cm) from the bottom of the container.

If the wick goes askew, you can just leave it alone and enjoy its wayward ways, or reheat the candle in a 175°F (80°C) oven until the gel melts. If the wick is an anchor wick, position it properly in the cooling gel and tug it taut to remove any slack that has developed. If you want a wick at the top, remove the wick before you reheat the candle. After the gel has melted and started to cool, re-insert the wick.

MAINTAIN THE WICK

Trimming the wick is not an option. You *have* to do it. A tall, exposed wick is a potential safety hazard because its large flame can generate enough heat to ignite the gel. Trim the wick to ¼ inch (6 mm) the first time you burn the candle. Then, every time you light the candle, make sure the wick is no taller than ¹⁄₁₆ inch (1.6 mm). Keep it short; keep it safe. To trim the wick, wait until the gel has cooled completely. Then turn the candle upside down, so no blackened bits of the wick will fall into the gel, and trim the wick with a pair of small scissors or nail clippers. Don't try to trim the wick while it's burning; the result will be a big mess.

Keeping a Notebook for Continued Success

As in any art, practice and consistency are the keys to gel candlemaking success. Achieving consistency is simple—keep a notebook! Record your pouring and cooling temperatures, how much dye, fragrance, and glitter you added, what you learned about placing the embeds and the wicks, and any other tips you want to be able to find quickly later. The notebook doesn't have to be anything fancy (it'll probably be spotted with gel globs anyway!), just something that is easy to write in and to keep handy with your candlemaking equipment.

The Projects

Our projects were designed to accentuate the gel itself, emphasizing its unique beauty and adaptability as an artistic medium. We wanted the projects to be easy enough for beginners to make—and provide a wide variety of techniques to inspire experienced candlemakers. We hope *Fantastic Gel Candles* encourages you to have as much fun as we did!

Lots of Little Squares

Designer
TERRY TAYLOR

It couldn't be easier to create this eye-catching display of simple square glass containers filled with gels of brilliant colors. The short, sturdy shapes make safe candles for use outdoors.

What You Need

Small glass containers

Pan

Clip-on pan thermometer

Candle gel wax

Gel dyes in bright colors

Metal spoon

Ladle

Wicks

Instructions

I   In a pan placed over low heat, melt enough gel to fill one of the containers, heating the gel to the highest temperature recommended by the manufacturer. Use the thermometer to make sure the gel doesn't get too hot. Gradually add a few chips or drops of dye, and stir gently with the metal spoon until you get the intense color you want.

2   When the temperature of the gel is as high as it should be, ladle the gel into the container.

3   Repeat steps 1 and 2 to prepare and pour the other colors.

4   When the gel is almost cool, insert the wicks.

Design Tip

Keep small glass containers handy in your candlemaking area, so you'll always have some ready to be filled with leftover colored gel.

VARIATION

Jewel-Tone Trio

Deep, rich red, blue, and green are favorite colors for three-part designs.

Designer
ALLISON SMITH

Vintage Charmers

Designer
ALLISON SMITH

The designs on vintage glasses are so charming,
you don't need to do anything to make
beautiful candles except pour the gel and
insert a wick. Delicate, nostalgic hints of dye
recall peaceful yesterdays.

What You Need

Glasses with pretty designs

Pan

Clip-on pan thermometer

Candle gel wax

Gel dye, any complementary color

Metal spoon

Wicks

Instructions

1   In a pan placed over low heat, melt enough gel to fill the glasses, heating the gel to the highest temperature recommended by the manufacturer. Use the thermometer to make sure the gel doesn't get too hot. Add just enough dye to lightly tint the gel, stirring gently with a metal spoon.

2   When the temperature of the gel is as high as it should be, pour the gel into the containers.

3   After the gel has cooled, insert the wicks.

Design Tip
Don't worry about bubbles—they aren't noticeable in containers with designs.

Safety Tip
Don't use vintage glasses that are chipped or cracked—they can shatter with the high heat of the gel.

Petite Suite

Designer
MEGAN KIRBY

Bargain bins in antique stores are great places to find lovely gel candle containers, such as these French-made engraved glasses.

Glass Pebbles

Easy-to-make and fun to show off—this is a pebble candle with an attitude! No matter where you put it, it will take center stage.

Designer
TERRY TAYLOR

What You Need

Glass container
Pan
Clip-on pan thermometer
Candle gel wax
Gel dye, blue
Metal spoon
Bubble stick
Wick
Flat-backed glass pebbles
Hot-glue gun and glue sticks

Instructions

1   In a pan placed over low heat, melt enough gel to fill the glass container, heating the gel to the highest temperature recommended by the manufacturer. Use the thermometer to make sure the gel doesn't get too hot. Gradually add a few chips or drops of blue dye, stirring gently with the metal spoon, until you get the color you want.

2   When the temperature of the gel is as high as it should be, pour the gel into the container. Use the bubble stick to reduce bubbles, if desired. When the gel is almost cool, insert the wick.

3   Apply a little hot glue to the backs of the pebbles and carefully press them against the glass. Start at the top of the container and work your way down the sides.

Design Tip

Many pretty, flat-backed objects that may melt in hot gel—such as shiny plastic cabochons, silk flowers, or ribbon—can be put to wonderful use as decorations on the outer surfaces of gel candle containers.

Simply Sequins

Designer
TERRY TAYLOR

Gel candles in groups are so lovely, that if they need any gilding at all, the simplest decoration is best. Small sequins bedeck the rims of these plain-Jane drinking glasses and transform them into sparkling aquamarine beauties.

Candle gel wax

Gel dye, turquoise

Metal spoon

Hot-glue gun and glue sticks

Wicks

Instructions

1   Invert a glass onto paper and trace around the rim. Arrange sequins around the traced circle to help determine how many sequins you'll need and where to place them.

2   In a pan placed over low heat, melt enough gel to fill the containers, heating the gel to the highest temperature recommended by the manufacturer. Use the thermometer to make sure the gel doesn't get too hot. Add just enough turquoise dye to lightly tint the gel, and stir gently with the metal spoon.

3   When the temperature of the gel is as high as it should be, pour the gel into the containers.

4   When the gel is almost cool, insert the wicks.

5   When the gel is completely cool, hot glue the sequins around the rim of each glass.

Design Tip
There are all kinds of shiny metal glue-ons at craft stores that will help you turn your ordinary glassware into fantastic gel candles.

What You Need

Glass containers

Paper

Pencil

Sequins

Pan

Clip-on pan thermometer

Bubbly Aquarium

Designer
ALLISON SMITH

Bubbles and more bubbles—and each one looks right at home in this big gel aquarium candle. Glass fish in sun-drenched tropical colors seem to swim forever.

What You Need

Aquarium or clear glass container

Measuring cup

Blue craft sand

Small seashells

Pan

Clip-on pan thermometer

Candle gel wax

Ladle

Glass fish or other glass sea creatures

Sewing thread

Bamboo skewers

Adhesive tape

Bubble stick

Dish towels

Wicks

Instructions

1   Fill the aquarium with water and measure the amount with a measuring cup to determine how much gel you'll need. The large candle shown here required almost 1 gallon (3.8 l) of gel. Dry the container completely.

2   Pour a layer of blue craft sand on the bottom of the aquarium. Stud the sand with small colorful shells.

3   In a pan placed over low heat, melt enough gel to fill the aquarium, heating the gel to the highest temperature recommended by the manufacturer. Use the thermometer to make sure the gel doesn't get too hot. Using a ladle, pour a 1-inch-thick (2.5 cm) layer of the hot gel over the sand to seal it. Allow the gel to cool completely.

4   While the gel is cooling, suspend the fish at dif-ferent heights against the inside aquarium walls by looping lengths of thread through them and tying the threads to bamboo skewers placed across the aquarium's top. Tape the skewers to the outside of the aquarium to hold them in place.

5   Return the gel in the pan to pouring temperature and ladle the very hot gel into the aquarium. Pour quickly, taking care to keep the fish in position.

6   Stir the gel with the bubble stick. To reduce the number of bubbles, wrap the aquarium with dish towels, which will slow down the cooling process. When the gel is almost cool, insert the wicks.

Design Tip

A big aquarium has more impact when you use a lot of fish, so don't be skimpy with the fish—or should that be scampi?!

Safety Tips

The glass panels of this aquarium are rimmed with plastic, so you can't heat the aquarium in the oven to reduce the bubbling. If you insist on having a bubble-free candle, use an all-glass container that you can heat in the oven. Also, a gel aquarium this size weighs more than 7 pounds (3 kg) so make sure you place it on something sturdy.

Lavender Glitter Stars

Designer
CORINNE KURZMANN

What You Need

Metal foil stars
Clear glass container
Tweezers
Metal skewer
Candle gel wax
Small bowl
Anchor wick
Pan
Clip-on pan thermometer
Lavender cosmetic glitter (optional)
Metal spoon

Tiny lavender stars
twinkle in a
"sweet dreams" candle.

Instructions

1   Press the stars against the inside walls of the container. The stars may stick just by static cling. If not, use the tweezers or metal skewer to dab each star with hot gel and press it against the glass. (Yes, this requires patience, but after the first few stars, it's easy.)

2   Attach the anchor wick, as the designer did. (Or insert it from the top after completing step 4.)

3   In a pan placed over low heat, melt enough clear gel to fill the container, heating the gel to the highest temperature recommended by the manufacturer. Use the thermometer to make sure the gel doesn't get too hot. Add a pinch of lavender cosmetic glitter, and stir thoroughly with the metal spoon.

4   Gently pour the gel into the container. Re-position any of the stars, if needed, with the metal skewer.

Design Tip
Don't use soapmaking glitter—it isn't shiny enough for gel candles.

Safety Tip
Keep glitter stars at least 1 inch (2.5 cm) away from the wick.

Mini Tree Lights

Charming, colorful, and clever—this candle is so appealing you'll never grow tired of looking at it! The tiny lightbulbs spiral through the clear gel, as if they were dancing.

Designer
TERRY TAYLOR

What You Need

Clear glass container

Scrap wire

Measuring tape or ruler

Package of tiny colored lightbulbs

18- or 20-gauge (1.00 or .75 mm) colored craft wire

Wire cutters

Pan

Clip-on pan thermometer

Candle gel wax

Metal skewer

Wick

Instructions

1   Shape a piece of scrap wire into a spiral to fit the container. Remove it, measure it, and double its length to determine how much wire you'll need to make the finished double-strand spiral.

2   Thread one of the bulbs onto one of the strands. Twist both strands to secure it in place. Continue twisting the wire for about 1 inch (2.5 cm) and slide another bulb onto one of the strands. Repeat until the strand is filled with bulbs. Fit the spiral inside the container, using wire cutters to trim the wires, if necessary.

3   In a pan placed over low heat, melt enough clear gel to fill the container, heating the gel to the highest temperature recommended by the manufacturer. Use the thermometer to make sure the gel doesn't get too hot. Let the gel cool slightly and then pour it gently into the container, being careful not to disturb the lights.

4   Make sure the wire is placed away from the wick. Use the metal skewer to adjust it, if necessary. When the gel is almost cool, insert a wick.

Design Tip
Make other candles for use any time of year—with beads, bells, charms, medals—any intriguing objects you can string on wire.

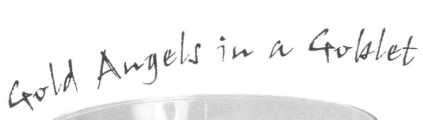

Gold Angels in a Goblet

Gold cherubs are perfectly heavenly in this glittery holiday goblet. Gold ribbon adds a merry touch.

Designer
ALLISON SMITH

What You Need

Glass container

Gold angel charms

Sewing thread

Adhesive tape

Pan

Clip-on pan thermometer

Candle gel wax

Gold gel glitter

Metal spoon

Metal skewer

Wick

Suspend charms at different heights.

Instructions

1   Arrange the angels to determine how many you'll need for your design.

2   Loop lengths of thread through the holes in the angel charms and suspend them at different heights inside the goblet. Tape each thread to the outside of the glass with adhesive tape. (See photo, lower left.) Make sure that the front of each charm faces out.

3   In a pan placed over low heat, melt enough gel to fill the goblet, heating the gel to the highest temperature recommended by the manufacturer. Use the thermometer to make sure the gel doesn't get too hot. With the metal spoon, gently stir in two small pinches of gold gel glitter. Carefully pour the gel mixture into the goblet. Reposition the charms, if necessary, with a metal skewer.

4   When the gel is cool, unfasten the taped thread ends and gently tug to remove them. Tiny thread-lines will remain in the gel, but they're almost invisible. Insert the wick.

Design Tip

You can find metal charms in many places—arts and crafts supply stores, gift shops, garage sales, and flea markets. A collection of charms with a theme, such as heart charms, military medals, or holiday ornaments, is most appealing.

Guardian Angel

A tiny silver ornament takes on guardian angel proportions, thanks to the effects of perspective through the round walls of the container. From a front window, the candle's midnight blue glow welcomes holiday travelers home.

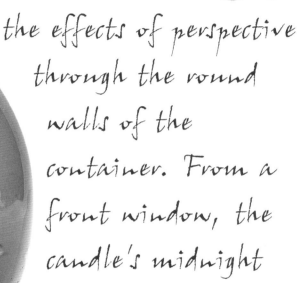

Designer
ALLISON SMITH

What You Need

Oven
Glass container
Seed beads, silver or pearl
Pan
Clip-on pan thermometer
Candle gel wax
Gel dye, blue
Metal spoon
Angel ornament: metal, ceramic, or glass
Baking dish
Wick

Instructions

1   Preheat the oven to 175°F (80°C).

2   On the bottom of the container, spread a layer of silver or pearl seed beads, at least $^1/_2$ inch (1.3 mm) thick.

3   In a pan placed over low heat, melt enough gel to fill the container, heating the gel to the highest temperature recommended by the manufacturer. Use the thermometer to make sure the gel doesn't get too hot. Gradually add a few chips or drops of dye, stirring gently with the metal spoon, until you get a very pale blue. (If the color is too dark it will hide the angel.)

4   Place the candle in an uncovered baking dish in the preheated oven for two hours, or until the bubbles have almost disappeared. A few bubbles are acceptable, but too many will detract from the angel, so you'll want to make this candle as bubble-free as possible.

5   Remove the candle and set it on a safe, flat, heat-resistant surface. When it's almost cool, insert a short wick.

Design Tip

No one is ever too grown-up for a guardian angel. This candle would be a perfect gift for a college student going away to school.

Perspective

The shape of a round glass container can cause light to refract and distort the appearance of an object in the center of the container. For example, this tiny ceramic teapot looks huge and misshapen in the "mistake" candle below. To decrease distortion of embeds in the center of a globe candle, use very small embeds and large containers. Or use flat embeds placed against the sides of the container, because objects closer to the glass suffer less distortion.

Bold Spirals

Bold-colored spirals and goblets with elegantly curved stems create a candle display that is perfectly at home with lace tablecloths and fine china.

What You Need

Goblets with lovely stems and wide shallow bowls

Measuring tape

Cookie sheet

Aluminum foil

Spray oil

Pan

Clip-on pan thermometer

Candle gel wax

Gel dye, blue

Metal spoon

Pizza cutter

Utility knife

Wicks

Design Tip

For a striking effect, experiment with strips made with two colors, such as red polka dots on green, or candy stripes in red and iridescent white.

Instructions

1 Measure the depth of the goblet bowls to determine how wide you need to cut the strips of gel. For example, these goblets required a gel strip $3/4$ inch (1.9 cm) wide.

2 Cover the cookie sheet with a piece of aluminum foil, putting the shiny side face up. Lightly spray it with oil so the gel will be easy to pull off.

3 In a pan placed over low heat, melt enough gel to make a $1/4$-inch-thick (6 mm) layer, heating the gel to the highest temperature recommended by the manufacturer. Use the thermometer to make sure the gel doesn't get too hot. Gradually add chips or drops of dye, stirring gently with a metal spoon, until you get the intense color you want.

4 Pour the gel carefully onto the cookie sheet. Let it cool completely.

5 With the pizza cutter, cut long strips of gel $3/4$ inch (1.9 cm) wide. Place each strip in a goblet and shape it into a swirl, starting at the center and working out towards the sides. With the utility knife, trim the lengths as needed. Depending on your design, you could use as much as 12 inches (30.5 cm) of gel in each of these goblets. The gel strips will stick easily to the bottom of the goblet bowls. Handle the gel strips carefully, but if you should tear one, just add it to your stock of leftover colored gel to use in other projects.

6 In a pan placed over low heat, melt enough clear gel to fill the container—but don't get it as hot as you would ordinarily because you don't want the gel to melt the colored swirls. Just heat it until it is pourable but not completely liquid. Pour the gel into the goblets. When the gel is almost cool, insert the wicks.

Winter Solstice Spiral

Celebrate the winter solstice with an updated version of an ancient symbol of Nature's renewal— the timeless spiral.

Designer
TERRY TAYLOR

What You Need

4 silver "chenille" pipe cleaners

Small bowl

Candle gel wax

Tweezers

Small clear glass container

Pan

Clip-on pan thermometer

Bubble stick

Wick

Instructions

1   Starting at the center and working outwards, shape the pipe cleaners into spirals that fit onto the walls of the glass.

2   Pre-treat the spirals by coating them with hot gel in a small bowl. Remove the pieces one by one, and run your fingers down their sides to wipe off the excess gel and let it drip off into the bowl.

3   Press each spiral lightly against the inner glass walls, spacing them as desired. Use the tweezers, if necessary. The little bit of gel that clings to the spirals helps adhere them to the glass.

4   In a pan placed over low heat, melt enough clear gel to fill the container, heating the gel to the highest temperature recommended by the manufacturer. Use the thermometer to make sure the gel doesn't get too hot, and pour it into the container. Bubbles look fine in this design, but if you want fewer of them, gently swirl the bubble stick in the gel.

5   When the gel is almost cool, insert a wick.

Jingle Bells

Ring in winter cheer with this pretty jingle bell candle.

Designer
TERRY TAYLOR

Design Tip
An embed placed in the center of a container often seems greatly enlarged—so choose your bell size carefully.

What You Need

Metal bell
Clear glass container
Small bowl
Candle gel wax
Thread
Bamboo skewer
Adhesive tape
Pan
Clip-on pan thermometer
Wick
Hot-glue gun and glue sticks
Ribbon with sewn-on bells

Instructions

1 Pre-treat the bell with melted gel in a small bowl.

2 Loop a length of thread through the hanger on the bell, so that the bell rests just below the middle of the container. Tie the thread to a bamboo skewer placed across the container's top. Tape the skewer to the outside of the container to hold it in place.

3 In a pan placed over low heat, melt enough clear gel to fill the container, heating the gel to the highest temperature recommended by the manufacturer. Use the thermometer to make sure the gel doesn't get too hot.

4 When the gel is almost cool, unfasten the thread ends and gently tug to remove them. Insert the wick.

5 When the gel is completely cool, hot glue the decorated ribbon to the container.

Snowy Stars

Like snow in moonlight, these candles glisten pearly white. The secret is lots of iridescent gel glitter and a simple, shiny ribbon.

Designer
ALLISON SMITH

What You Need

Glass container

Pan

Clip-on pan thermometer

Candle gel wax

Iridescent gel glitter

Metal spoon

Wick

Ribbon

Embroidered star appliqué

Hot-glue gun and glue sticks

VARIATION

Candy Dish Surprises

Designers
ALLISON SMITH and
TERRY TAYLOR

Instructions

1   In a pan placed over low heat, melt enough gel to fill the container, heating the gel to the highest temperature recommended by the manufacturer. Use the thermometer to make sure the gel doesn't get too hot.

2   Add 1 heaping teaspoon of iridescent gel glitter to the gel. Stir gently with the metal spoon to make the gel opaque and snowy, and pour it into the container.

3   When the gel is almost cool, insert the wick.

4   When the gel is completely cool, hot glue the ribbon and the star to the container.

Design Tip
Holiday candles look especially nice in group arrangements with containers of various sizes and soft, wintry shades of gel.

A hint of iridescent glitter adds shimmer to the surprise—when you take off the lids and discover gel candles inside!

Zen Rock Garden

The utter simplicity of this candle is a pleasure to the eye, a subtle invitation to be still and look inward. The clear gel accentuates the natural beauty of the river pebbles.
Four wicks emphasize balance.

Designer
TERRY TAYLOR

What You Need

Wide square glass container with thick walls
Oven
Cookie sheet
Aluminum foil
Pan
Clip-on pan thermometer
River pebbles
Candle gel wax
Wicks

Instructions

1   Choose a wide square container with thick glass walls that can bear the weight of the pebbles.

2   Make sure that your oven rack is level. Pour water into the container, set it on the rack, and observe it at eye level. If the layer is not level, adjust the container with supports of folded aluminum foil. Remove the container from the oven and dry it thoroughly.

3   Pre-heat the oven to 175°F (80°C).

4   Wash the pebbles and let them dry completely to remove all traces of water or residue that could make the gel cloudy. Arrange the pebbles in a layer on the bottom of the container.

5   In a pan placed over low heat, melt enough gel to fill the container to the highest temperature recommended by the manufacturer. Use the thermometer to make sure the gel doesn't get too hot. Pour the gel over the pebbles.

6   Place the candle in the pre-heated oven for several hours to cool slowly and to remove as many bubbles as possible. Be careful to hold the container level when you carry it, so the gel layer will be perfectly straight.

7   When the gel is almost cool, insert the four wicks.

Design Tip
Other objects that make stunning bottom layers are glass pebbles, marbles, tumbled glass, and coins.

Kitchen Quartet

Colorful pasta and dried foods combine with the pretty shape of small wine carafes to make a homey kitchen candle display.

What You Need

Glass carafes or other tall containers

Dried foods ingredients such as corn, beans, and pasta

Pan

Clip-on pan thermometer

Candle gel wax

Wick

Designer
THERESA GWYNN

Instructions

1 Fill the containers with the dried foods, packing them tightly against the glass walls so there are no gaps. A solid wall of colors and shapes is pleasing to the eye.

2 In a pan placed over low heat, melt enough gel to fill the containers, heating the gel to the highest temperature recommended by the manufacturer. Use the thermometer to make sure the gel doesn't get too hot. Pour the gel into the carafes, over the dried foods.

3 When the gel is almost cool, insert a short wick into each container. Keep the wicks at least 1 inch (2.5 cm) from the dried foods.

Design Tip

Not all dried foods will work with gel, so plan on experimenting. Try black rice, dried cranberries, sunflower seeds, and other ingredients with different colors and shapes.

Spices in Mason Jars

Clear gel brings out the rich, earthy colors and fascinating natural shapes of cinnamon and star anise. With their tight-fitting lids, Mason jars make excellent candle containers to pack and send to long-distance friends.

Designer
CORINNE KURZMANN

What You Need

Cinnamon sticks
Star anise
Mason jars in different sizes
Bowl
Candle gel wax
Tweezers
Pan
Clip-on pan thermometer
Metal skewer (optional)
Wick

Instructions

1 Determine how many sticks of cinnamon and pieces of star of anise will look best in your design. Cut cinnamon sticks, if necessary, to fit the jar.

2 Pre-treat the cinnamon and star anise by coating them with hot gel in a bowl . When the gel has stopped bubbling, remove the ingredients with tweezers. Wait about 30 seconds for the items to cool, then wipe them down with your fingers to allow excess gel to drip back into the saucer. Discard this gel. Natural objects can release oil, which will make the gel murky and unusable for candles.

3 In a pan placed over low heat, melt enough gel to fill the jars, heating the gel to the highest temperature recommended by the manufacturer. Use the thermometer to make sure the gel doesn't get too hot. Pour the gel into the jars.

4 Insert the cinnamon sticks in the taller jar so they are resting on the bottom and angled attractively against the sides.

5 When the gel has cooled slightly in the short jar, use tweezers or a metal skewer to position the star anise.

6 To help the candles cool slowly, cover each of them with a saucer. When the gel is almost cool, insert the wicks.

Design Tip
Mason jar candles make welcome housewarming gifts. Add raffia or a ribbon for a personal touch.

Crystals in Clear Gel

Designer
CORRINE KURZMANN

Like tiny jewel icebergs, these amethyst crystals seem to rise out of a clear sea. When the candle is lit and the flame reflects off the crystals, it takes on a magical, otherworldly look. In such a shallow dish, the flame will be brief— but oh—so beautiful!

What You Need

Container with a wide, shallow dish

Oven

Cookie sheet

Aluminum foil

Crystals of various shapes and heights

Anchor wick

Pan

Clip-on pan thermometer

Candle gel wax

Design Tip

With a shallow layer of gel, the candle can't burn for very long. But you can easily remove the old wick, refresh the layer of gel and re-heat it in the oven, if necessary. The heat won't hurt the crystals.

Instructions

1   Make sure that your oven rack is level. Pour water into the container, set it on a cookie sheet on the rack, and observe it at eye level. If the layer is not level, adjust the container with supports of folded aluminum foil. Remove the container from the oven and dry thouroughly.

2   Pre-heat the oven to 175°F (80°C).

3   Carefully choose the crystals and decide how you want to arrange them before you place them in the gel. An uneven number of crystals (three, five, or seven) looks best.

4   Attach an anchor wick to the bottom of the container as the designer did, or insert it from the top after step 5.

5   In a pan placed over low heat, melt enough clear gel to fill the container, heating the gel to the highest temperature recommended by the manufacturer. Use the thermometer to make sure the gel doesn't get too hot. Pour a thin layer of gel into the container.

6   Firmly press the crystals into the gel so their bottoms are securely seated in the gel. Carefully, add more gel so it reaches just below the top of the container.

7   Place the candle on the cookie sheet in the pre-heated oven for several hours to cool slowly and reduce bubbling. (If you want a different, equally attractive look, leave the bubbles in.)

Seashells on Sand

Sea-washed shells imbue this candle with fantasies of far away beaches. Unplug the computer, throw away the cell phone—it's time to be languorous and do nothing.

Designer
ALLISON SMITH

What You Need

Wide, shallow, clear glass container

Oven

Cookie sheet

Aluminum foil

White or beige craft sand

Seashells

Candle gel wax

Wide bowl

Tweezers

Pan

Clip-on pan thermometer

Ladle

Wick

Instructions

1   Make sure that your oven rack is level. Pour water into the container, set it on a cookie sheet on the rack, and observe it at eye level. If the layer is not level, adjust the container with supports of folded aluminum foil. Remove the container from the oven and dry thoroughly.

2   Pre-heat the oven to 175°F (80°C).

3   Clean the shells and allow them to dry completely.

4   Pre-treat the shells by coating them with hot gel in a large bowl. Use the tweezers to remove them and allow any excess gel to drip back into the bowl.

5   Place a layer of sand on the bottom of the container and carefully place the shells in the sand.

6   In a pan placed over low heat, melt enough gel to fill the container, heating the gel to the highest temperature recommended by the manufacturer. Use the thermometer to make sure the gel doesn't get too hot. Ladle the hot gel over the shells. Pour enough gel over the shells to create a pleasant amount of space between the gel and the rim of the container.

7   Place the candle in the pre-heated oven for at least 5 hours. Turn off the oven and let the container cool down slowly in the oven overnight. When it has cooled completely, insert the wick.

Design Tip

For a bolder look, arrange different colored layers of colored craft sand, such as sky blue,

Colored Craft Sand

Craft sands are wonderful additions to gel candles, whether you use them as design elements by alternating layers of sand and gel, or as accents for scenic candles. After you add the gel, the sand will usually look several shades darker than it did in the package. You can lighten craft sand before pouring the gel by mixing it with beach sand, or create new colors by mixing several colors together.

Costume Jewelry Flower Garden

Designer
TERRY TAYLOR

Costume jewelry flowers dazzle as embeds in a small "garden" gel candle. The gold metal finish on the backs of the flowers is magnified by the effects of perspective, adding an unexpected element of sparkle.

What You Need

Assortment of costume jewelry
in flower designs

Candle gel wax

Small bowl

Tweezers

Clear glass container

Pan

Clip-on pan thermometer

Ladle

Metal skewer

Bubble stick

Wick

Instructions

I   Remove any clips, posts, or pin backs on the jewelry. Clean and dry the jewelry pieces thoroughly and pre-treat them by coating them with clear melted gel in a small bowl. Remove the pieces one by one, and press them lightly in a row against the inner glass wall at the bottom of the container. Use the tweezers to push them against the glass, if necessary. The little bit of gel that clings to the jewelry pieces will help adhere them to the glass.

2   In a pan placed over low heat, melt enough fresh gel to fill the container, heating the gel to the highest temperature recommended by the manufacturer. Use the thermometer to make sure the gel doesn't get too hot. Let the gel cool slightly before ladling it into the container. If a piece of jewelry should slip away from the glass wall, re-position it with the metal skewer. Use the bubble stick to reduce bubbling, if needed, but be careful not to disturb the jewelry pieces

3   When the gel is almost cool, insert a wick.

Design Tip

For solid color jewelry flowers, a thin layer of "grassy" green gel on the container bottom adds a bright blade of color.

Musical Wires

The lyrical shapes of musical symbols add lovely "grace notes" to the strong lines of this gel candle. It would look perfect posing on a piano or in the window of a rehearsal room.

Designer
ALLISON SMITH

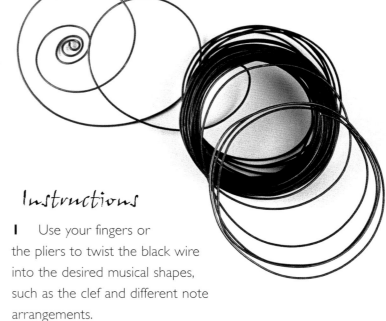

What You Need

18- or 20-gauge flexible black wire

Wire cutters

Round-nose or flat-nose pliers

Sewing thread

Tall, square glass container

Adhesive tape

Metal skewer

Pan

Clip-on pan thermometer

Candle gel wax

Gel dye, orange

Metal spoon

Wicks

Design Tip

Try your hand at making other wire shapes for gel candles, such as hearts, shamrocks, holiday ornaments, and religious symbols.

Instructions

1　Use your fingers or the pliers to twist the black wire into the desired musical shapes, such as the clef and different note arrangements.

2　Loop lengths of thread through the tops of the wire notes and suspend them at different heights inside the container. Tape each thread to the outside of the glass with adhesive tape. Using the metal skewer if needed, press the wire shapes firmly against the side of the container. (See the instructions in Gold Angels in a Goblet, page 38.)

3　In a pan placed over low heat, melt enough gel to fill the container, heating the gel to the highest temperature recommended by the manufacturer. Use the thermometer to make sure the gel doesn't get too hot. Gradually add a few chips or drops of dye, stirring gently with the metal spoon, until you get the color you want.

4　Carefully pour the gel into the container. If necessary, use the metal skewer to re-position the wire shapes.

5　When the gel is almost cool, unfasten the taped thread ends and gently tug up on them to remove the threads. Insert the wick.

Sunken Treasure

Rescue jewelry castaways in this seashore-themed candle. Seen through clear gel and nestled on black velvety sand, the sunken treasures gleam like a queen's ransom.

Designer
ALLISON SMITH

What You Need

Wide, shallow, clear glass container

Oven

Cookie sheet

Aluminum foil

Black craft sand

Assortment of costume jewelry in metal, glass, and ceramic

Candle gel wax

Pan

Clip-on pan thermometer

Ladle

Wick

Instructions

1   Make sure that your oven rack is level. Pour water into the container, set it on a cookie sheet on the rack, and observe it at eye level. If the rack is not level, adjust the container with supports of folded aluminum foil. Remove the container from the oven and dry thoroughly.

2   Pre-heat the oven to 175°F (80°C).

3   Place a layer of sand on the bottom of the dish and arrange the jewelry on it.

4   In a pan placed over low heat, melt enough gel to fill the container, heating the gel to the highest temperature recommended by the manufacturer. Use the thermometer to make sure the gel doesn't get too hot. Gently pour the heated gel over the jewelry in a layer at least 1 inch (2.5 m) thick.

5   Put the candle in the preheated oven for several hours to remove as many bubbles as possible while the gel cools slowly. A wide-dish candle may be heavier than you expect, so be careful to hold it level when you carry it to the oven, so the gel layer will be perfectly straight.

6   When the gel is almost cool, insert a short wick, no closer than 1 inch (2.5 cm) from any piece of jewelry.

Design Tip
Use jewelry pieces with different shapes and colors. Lay them out ahead of time to see which combination works best.

Fiery Copper Wire Candle

Brimming to the edges with copper wire, this brandy snifter candle seems to burst with electrical charges. Place the candle unlit in a window and it glints all day. Light it at night, and it glows.

Designer
TERRY TAYLOR

What You Need

Spool of copper wire

Polystyrene ball to fit the container

Tweezers

Wire cutters

Round or curved glass container

Anchor wick

Pan

Clip-on pan thermometer

Candle gel wax

Instructions

I   Use one of the following methods to make the wire shape:

The Loose-Wrap Method
Loosely wrap the copper wire around the foam ball a few times to rough out the shape you want. Then gently push the ball out. (You might have to tug at the wires a bit and push them back into position afterwards.) Continue wrapping and pressing the wire until it has the shape you want.

The Tight-Wrap Method
Wind the wire around the foam ball a few times to start the wire frame. With tweezers or wire cutters, chop out the ball in pieces. Continue wrapping to get your final shape.

2   Fit the wire shape into the container. Anchor a wick in the container. Spread apart the wires at the top so they won't touch the wick.

3   In a pan placed over low heat, melt enough gel to fill the container, heating the gel to the highest temperature recommended by the manufacturer. Use the thermometer to make sure the gel doesn't get too hot. Pour the gel into the container.

Design Tip
For tall candles, make exciting wire spirals by wrapping wire around a pencil, or by bending and twisting wire into simple geo- metric shapes.

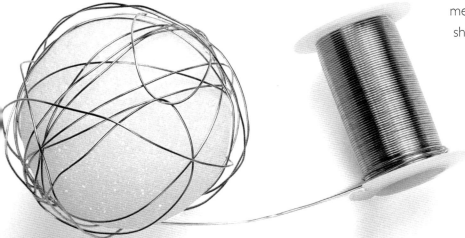

Mardi Gras Candle

A ceramic mask, lightning streaks of wire, beads of many colors—these simple candle elements capture the revelry and mystery of Mardi Gras.

Designer
TERRY TAYLOR

What You Need

Tall, clear glass container
Anchor wick
Assortment of colorful gel-compatible beads
Miniature ceramic mask with hanging holes
18- or 20- gauge (1.00 or .75 mm) copper and colored wire
Pencil
Wire cutters
Pan
Clip-on pan thermometer
Candle gel wax
Metal skewer
Bubble stick

Instructions

1   Attach an anchor wick to the bottom of the container, as our designer did, or insert one from the top after step 4. Add a layer of colorful beads.

2   Thread the wires through the holes in the mask. Shape the loose ends by wrapping them around a pencil. Don't worry about being too precise as you shape the wires—wildness looks good with this design. With the wire cutters, trim the ends.

3   Place the mask into the container at a jaunty angle. Be sure to keep the wires at the top away from the wick so they won't interfere with the flame.

4   In a pan placed over low heat, melt enough gel to fill the container, heating the gel to the highest temperature recommended by the manufacturer. Use the thermometer to make sure the gel doesn't get too hot. Pour the heated gel into the container. Bubbles look fine in this design, but if you want fewer of them, gently swirl the bubble stick in the gel, being careful not to disturb the beads or the mask. Or you can reheat the candle in a 175°F (80°C) oven for several hours.

Design Tip

Two matching candles with the traditional masks of tragedy and comedy embedded in them would be a perfect gift for theatre lovers.

Tower with Hoops of Beads

Designer
ALLISON SMITH

Layers of brilliantly colored gel and hoops of tumbled glass beads turn an easy-to-make candle into a breathtaking work of art. By the time you reach the top layer of this tower candle, your feelings of accomplishment will have soared as high as your imagination. Go for it!

What You Need

Tall, glass container

Measuring cup

Assortment of tumbled glass beads

18- or 20-gauge copper wire

Wire cutters

Pliers

Tape measure or ruler

Felt-tip marker

Pan

Clip-on pan thermometer

Candle gel wax

Gel dyes in compatible colors

Ladle

Metal skewer

Wick

Instructions

1　Fill your container with water and measure the amount with a measuring cup to determine how much gel you'll need. Then divide the total by the number of layers to determine how much you'll need for each layer. (This project took 2 quarts (1.9 L) of gel for all six layers.) Dry the container thoroughly.

2　Choose enough pretty beads to make the number of hoops you want in your design. (This design has five hoops.) Tumbled glass beads look lovely through the gel, but any pretty, gel-compatible beads will do. When using dark gel colors, you can't see the details of the beads, so choose beads with distinctive shapes.

3　String the beads onto the cooper wire and bend the wire into hoops. Fit each of the hoops inside the glass container to make sure it rests flat and fits snugly against the glass walls. Using the pliers, make a hook at each end of each wire and crimp the ends with the pliers to make a secure circle.

4   With the felt-tip marker, measure and mark off equidistant lines on one outside wall of the container to indicate the top of each layer. Use these marks to help you pour the gel and position the beaded hoops.

5   In a pan placed over low heat, melt enough gel for one layer, heating the gel to the highest temperature recommended by the manufacturer. Use the thermometer to make sure the gel doesn't get too hot. Gradually add a few chips or drops of dye until you get the color you want.

6   When the temperature of the gel is as high as it should be, ladle the gel into the container to the level indicated by the mark. To create distinctive lines between the layers, let the gel cool completely before adding the next layer.

7   When the gel is completely cool, place a beaded hoop on top of it. If necessary, use the metal skewers, to press it flat.

8   Repeat steps 5 to 7 with each of the different colored gel layers and beaded hoops. After you position the last hoop, pour in the final layer of colored gel.

9   When the last layer is almost cool, insert a wick about two layers in length.

10   When the candle has burned down too far to trim the wick easily, pull out the wick and add fresh layers of gel and a new wick.

Design Tip
Glass beads look translucent in the gel, so use a pretty wire that will show through them. If you use opaque beads, you won't see the wire, so any wire is fine.

Safety Tip
Don't be tempted to create a tall flame to match the tall container! Keep the wick trimmed to no more than $1/16$ inch (1.6 mm) after its first burn.

Jagged Edges

The incision technique creates an exciting candle with edges of distinction.

Designer
HEATHER SMITH

What You Need

Tall glass container
2 pans
Clip-on pan thermometer
Candle gel wax
Gel dye, fluorescent red
Metal spoon
Knife, with a long, thin blade
Wick

Instructions

1   In a pan placed over low heat, melt enough clear gel to fill the container, heating the gel to the highest temperature recommended by the manufacturer. Pour half the gel into the other pan. Then, fill one-third of the container with the hot clear gel. Set the container aside until the gel is completely cooled.

2   Re-heat the gel in the second pan. Add chunks of fluorescent red dye, stirring gently with the metal spoon, until you get the intense color you want.

3   When the clear gel layer in the container is cool, pour a layer of the red gel on top of it. While the red gel is still hot, use the knife and repeatedly pierce the red gel down through the layer of clear gel. The hot red gel will ooze into the incisions you made to form red spikes in the clear gel layer.

4   Repeat steps 1 to 3 to create the rest of the candle, alternating the layers of clear and red gel. When the top layer is almost cool, insert the wick.

Design Tip

The deeper the color of the dyed gel layer, the more it will stand out against the clear layer.

Two-Tone Teardrops

Designer
TERRY TAYLOR

Blue on green, red on black, purple on orange—the two-tone combinations in gel appliqués are limited only by your imagination.

What You Need

Glass container

Cookie sheet

Aluminum foil

Spray oil

Pan

Clip-on pan thermometer

Candle gel wax

Gel candle dye, blue and green

Iridescent gel glitter

Metal spoon

Cookie cutters, teardrop and small circle

Wick

Instructions

1   If you have leftover colored gel, use it for the cutouts and start with step 6.

2   Cover the cookie sheet with aluminum foil, placing the shiny side face up. Lightly spray it with the oil so the gel will be easy to pull off. If you're going to make only one candle and don't need a lot of gel for cutouts, then cut and fold the aluminum foil to make small flat-bottomed "trays" to hold the gel. (See Making Appliqués of Color on page 17.)

3   In a pan placed over low heat, melt enough gel to make a ¼-inch-thick (6 mm) layer of gel on the cookie sheet, heating the gel to the highest temperature recommended by the manufacturer. Use the thermometer to make sure the gel doesn't get too hot. Gradually add a few drops or chips of dye, stirring gently with the metal spoon, until you get the color you want.

4   Pour the gel carefully onto one section of the cookie sheet. Let it cool completely.

5   Repeat steps 3 and 4 for the second color.

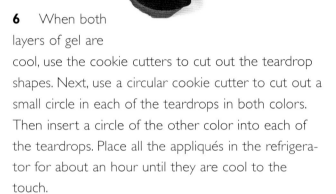

6   When both layers of gel are cool, use the cookie cutters to cut out the teardrop shapes. Next, use a circular cookie cutter to cut out a small circle in each of the teardrops in both colors. Then insert a circle of the other color into each of the teardrops. Place all the appliqués in the refrigerator for about an hour until they are cool to the touch.

7   Gently press each of the completed teardrop appliqués against the inner walls of the container. They'll stick easily.

8   In a pan placed over low heat, melt enough clear gel to fill the container, but don't heat the gel to as high a temperature as you would ordinarily, or it will melt the colored gel appliqués. Just heat the gel until it is pourable, but not completely liquid. Add two pinches of iridescent gel glitter and stir gently with the metal spoon. Pour the gel into the container.

9   When the gel is almost cool, insert the wick.

Design Tip
Glitter-enhanced gel, such as iridescent white, brings out the color in dyed gel appliqués and makes the bubbles less noticeable, too.

Flower Power

The sock-it-to-you orange and purple colors of the flower appliqués make them pop out of the clear gel background.

Designer
ALLISON SMITH

What You Need

Glass container

Cookie sheet

Aluminum foil

Spray oil

Pan

Clip-on pan thermometer

Candle gel wax

Gel candle dye, orange and purple

Metal spoon

Cookie cutters, large and small flowers

Bubble stick (optional)

Wick

Design Tip

Over time, embedded color appliqués will bleed slightly, and their edges will soften. The candle won't be as bold as it first was, but it will still be quite pretty.

Instructions

1 If you have leftover colored gel, use it for the cutouts and start with step 5.

2 Cover the cookie sheet with aluminum foil, placing the shiny side face up. Lightly spray it with the oil so the gel will be easy to pull off. If you're only going to make one candle and don't need a lot of gel for cutouts, then make "trays" to hold each color of dye. (See Making Appliqués of Color on page 17.)

3 In a pan placed over low heat, melt enough gel to make a ¼-inch-thick (6 mm) layer of gel on the cookie sheet, heating the gel to the highest temperature recommended by the manufacturer. Use the thermometer to make sure the gel doesn't get too hot. Gradually add a few drops or chips of dye, stirring gently with the metal spoon, until you get the color you want.

4 Pour the gel carefully onto one section of the cookie sheet. Let it cool completely. Repeat steps 3 and 4 for the second color.

6 When both layers are completely cool, use cookie cutters to cut out the flower appliqués. Then place the appliqués in the refrigerator for about an hour until they're cool to the touch.

7 Gently pick up and press each flower cutout against the side of the container. They'll stick easily.

8 In a pan placed over low heat, melt enough clear gel to fill the container, but don't heat the gel to as high a temperature as you would ordinarily, or it will melt the colored gel appliqués. Just heat the gel until it is pourable but not completely liquid. Pour the gel into the container. Use a bubble stick if you wish to reduce any bubbling.

9 When the candle is almost cool, insert the wick.

VARIATION

Fairy Flower Pots

Tiny flower cut-outs in tiny clear glass pots—another fantastic way to use leftover gel.

Designer
VERONIKA GUNTER

Tower of Pizzazz

Designer
ALLISON SMITH

Big, bold, and beautiful—this candle is a straight-up tower of style and pizzazz! Shorter versions take less gel and time to make, but are just as snazzy.

What You Need

Paper

Colored pencils or markers

Tall, glass container

Tape measure or ruler

Felt-tip marker

2 pans

Clip-on pan thermometer

Candle gel wax

Gel dyes, green, orange or purple

Metal spoon

Wick

Instructions

1   Sketch your design and colors on paper. Measure the glass container, and with a felt-tip marker, mark off the starting lines of each layer. For example, the container in this project is 11 inches (27.9 cm) tall. Each colored layer is about 1¼ inches (3.2 cm) deep. Each clear layer is about 2 inches (5.1 cm) deep. The lines on the outside of the glass will help you see how much gel you need to pour.

2   In a pan placed over low heat, melt enough gel for all of the clear gel layers, heating the gel to the highest temperature recommended by the manufacturer. Use the thermometer to make sure the gel doesn't get too hot. Using the first line on the container as a guide, pour the first layer to the mark. Allow the gel to cool completely.

3   In another pan placed over low heat, melt enough gel to create one of the colored layers. Gradually add a few chips or drops of dye, stirring gently with the metal spoon, until you get the color you want.

4   Using the next line on the container as a guide, pour the colored gel layer. Allow it to cool completely.

5   Clean out the pan that held the colored dye, keeping any leftover gel for use in other projects.

6   Repeat steps 2 to 5 as necessary, allowing each layer to cool completely before pouring the next layer. When the top clear layer is almost cool, insert a wick.

Design Tips

Yes, you're right: it can take all day for all the layers in this project to cool completely. Budget your time accordingly. You can decrease the cooling time by putting the candle in the refrigerator. Just remember not to pour the next layer of hot gel into a cold container. Allow the container to warm up in a 140°F (60°C) oven for about 10 minutes.

Even a few colored layers make beautiful candles.

Too-Much-Fun Tower

Designer
HEATHER SMITH

It's goofy, it's clever, it's totally too much fun! The fluorescent green, blue, and pink keep the candle summer-vacation-cheery any time of year.

What You Need

Interestingly shaped, tall glass container
1 large pan
3 small pans
Clip-on pan thermometer
Candle gel wax
Fluorescent gel dyes: blue, green, and red
Metal spoon
3 turkey basters
Wick

Instructions

1   In a large pan placed over low heat, melt enough clear gel to fill the container. Pour about a cup of gel into each of the three small pans. Use the thermometer to make sure the gel doesn't get too hot.

2   Dye the gel in each of the three small pans. Add the dye a little at a time, stirring gently with the metal spoon, until you reach the color you want.

3   Re-heat the clear gel to the highest temperature recommended by the manufacturer and fill the container about one-third with the gel. Let the gel cool until it's firm.

4   Keep all of the pots warm so the gel remains fluid as you work.

5   Fill a turkey baster with one of the colored gels and insert it about 1 inch (2.5 cm) into the firm, clear gel in the container. To prevent the gel from dripping out of the baster before you're ready to squeeze it, don't hold the baster at an angle. If you hold it in a vertical position, the air pressure holds the gel in. Lightly squeeze the ball of the baster until a little gel starts to ooze from it. (See photograph to the right.) Then very slowly remove the baster as you continue to lightly squeeze out the colored gel.

6   Repeat step 5, using the two other colored gels and turkey basters to create floating orbs and globules in the clear gel.

7   Pour the rest of the clear gel into the container, and let it cool until firm.

8   Repeat steps 5 and 6 to decorate the top layer of clear gel.

9   When the top layer is almost cool, insert a wick.

Design Tips

Use a skewer to tease out any gel that has solidified inside the turkey baster.

Label the turkey basters so that you will only use them for candlemaking. Store them with the rest of your candlemaking supplies.

Polka Dot Delight

Designer
ALLISON SMITH

These playful polka dots are positively irresistible! And they're so easy to make, you'll want a chorus line in all kinds of dot colors.

What You Need

Glass goblet

Cookie sheet

Aluminum foil

Spray oil

Pan

Clip-on pan thermometer

Candle gel wax

Gel dye, blue

Metal spoon

Small circular cookie cutter

Wick

Instructions

1 If you have leftover colored gel, use it for the cutouts and start with step 5.

2 Cover the cookie sheet with aluminum foil, placing the shiny side face up. Lightly spray it with the oil so the gel will be easy to pull off. If you're only going to make one candle and don't need a lot of gel for cutouts, then make "trays" to hold each color of dye. (See Making Appliqués of Color on page 17.)

3 In a pan placed over low heat, melt enough gel to make a $1/4$-inch-thick (6 mm) layer of gel on the cookie sheet, heating the gel to the highest temperature recommended by the manufacturer. Use the thermometer to make sure the gel doesn't get too hot. Gradually add a few drops or chips of dye, stirring gently with the metal spoon, until you get the color you want.

8 When the gel is completely cool, insert the wick.

Design Tip

Don't overcrowd the dots. Leave them plenty of swimming space for a pleasing, airy look.

4 Pour the gel carefully onto one section of the cookie sheet. Let it cool completely.

5 Use the cookie cutter to cut out circles. Then place the dots in the refrigerator for about an hour until they're cool to the touch.

6 Gently press the dots against the side of the container. They'll stick easily.

7 In a pan placed over low heat, melt enough clear gel to fill the container, but don't heat the gel to as high a temperature as you would ordinarily, or it will melt the colored gel appliqués. Just heat the gel until it is pourable, but not completely liquid. Pour the gel into the container.

Floating Flowers Centerpiece

Designers
ALLISON SMITH and
TERRY TAYLOR

Rich, cranberry-colored flowers float in a crystal clear punchbowl. The cups add color and flickering flames that reflect on the sides of the bowl.

What You Need

Glass punch bowl and cups
Fluted muffin tins, 3 inches (7.6 cm) in diameter
Spray oil
Pan
Clip-on pan thermometer
Cranberry dye
Candle gel wax
Ladle
Glass baking dish
Punch bowl ladle for decoration

Instructions

1   Determine how much gel you'll need. If you'll be happy with one short dramatic flourish when the candles are first lit, then you'll need just enough gel for a grand opening. But if you want the floating candles to burn for a long time, plan on making extra sets so you can replace the used ones as needed throughout the party.

2   Spray the muffin tins with oil, so you can remove the gel easily later in step 6.

3   In a pan placed over low heat, melt the gel to the highest temperature recommended by the manufacturer. Use the thermometer to make sure the gel doesn't get too hot. Gradually add a few chips of cranberry dye until you get the color you want. Very dark colors require a lot of dye, so you may have to add more after testing.

4   When the temperature of the gel is as high as it should be, pour some of the gel into the glass cups.

5   Reheat the remaining gel to pouring temperature, if necessary. Using the ladle, pour this gel into the muffin tins. Fill some of the tins close to the top to make large flowers. Fill others only halfway to make smaller flowers.

6   When the gel in the tins has completely cooled, carefully slip the flower shapes out and onto a flat, smooth, nonporous surface, such as a glass baking dish, for safekeeping. To keep them perky, refrigerate the flowers on the baking dish until you need them.

7   Repeat steps 5 and 6 as many times as necessary to make the number of flower molds you want.

8   Cut as many wicks as you need for the flowers, in equal lengths of no more than $1/2$ inch (1.3 cm). Insert the wicks, working at eye level, if possible. Do not insert the wicks all the through the flowers—or they'll absorb water and won't light. Cut wicks for the cup candles and insert them.

9   Fill the punch bowl with water and carefully place the flowers so they float on the top. Arrange the cup candles and the punch bowl ladle.

Design Tip
Make flowers in different shades of the same color by adjusting the proportions of dye and gel.

Goblets with Gold and Pearls

Classic pearls and a sassy touch of gold create elegance in these companion goblets. They make the perfect candle duo for bridal showers, weddings, anniversaries, and other celebrations where you want a look of luxury.

Designer
ALLISON SMITH

What You Need

2 glass goblets

18- or 20- gauge (1.00 or .75 mm) wire

Large assortment of faux pearls

Pan

Clip-on pan thermometer

Candle gel wax

Gold leaf flakes

Metal skewer

Wick

Instructions

Wide Goblet

1   The wire isn't visible through the beads, so you can use any kind of flexible wire. Make a test coil with the wire to estimate how much wire and how many pearls you'll need. The coil shown here required about 3½ feet (1.1 m) of wire and more than 100 pearls.

2   Thread the pearls onto the wire. Starting at the center and working outwards, shape the wire into a spiral that fits into the goblet, with the outermost spiral resting against the walls of the goblet.

3   In a pan placed over low heat, melt enough clear gel to fill the goblet, heating the gel to the highest temperature recommended by the manufacturer.

Use the thermometer to make sure the gel doesn't get too hot. Pour the gel into the goblet.

4   After the gel has cooled a bit, add gold leaf flakes, using a metal skewer to position them throughout the gel. When the gel is almost cool, insert a short wick.

Tall Goblet

1   Drop a handful of pearls into the bottom of the goblet. About 20 were placed in the goblet shown.

2   In a pan placed over low heat, melt enough clear gel to fill the goblet, heating the gel to the highest temperature recommended by the manufacturer. Pour the gel into the goblet.

3   When the gel has cooled a bit, drop in a few more pearls and position them with the metal skewer so that they appear to float. Add some gold leaf flakes and position them with the skewer, too. Let the gel cool some more, then drop in a few more pearls and pieces of foil.

4   When the gel is completely cool, insert a short wick.

Design Tips

Plan on experimenting a little before you commit to making these candles for a scheduled event. It helps to have a little experience with gel when you make a candle that has "floating" embeds.

Safety Tip

Use sturdy glass goblets for gel candles, as hot gel can crack very thin glass.

Sensational Sushi

Designers
ALLISON SMITH and
TERRY TAYLOR

Your guests will be astounded when they
realize this tasty-looking appetizer plate is a
display of small gel candles! While you make
the individual elements of these candles, you'll
want to pay as much attention to details
as a sushi master does while preparing real
Japanese specialties.

What You Need

Pretty plate for the "sushi"

Matching bowl for "soy sauce"

Cookie tin

Aluminum foil

Spray oil

Pan

Clip-on pan thermometer

Candle gel wax

Gel dye: white, pink, fluorescent green, dark green, and brown

Iridescent gel glitter

Metal spoon

Pizza cutter

Sharp knife

Wicks

Instructions

To make the colored gel strips:

1   Cover the cookie sheet, placing the foil's shiny side face up. Then, using a double layer of foil, make four "trays" to hold each color of dye: cut the foil, fold up the sides, and fold and pinch the corners together. Depending upon the size of your cookie sheet, make three sections about 4 inches square (10.2 cm) and make the last one, for the "nori" about 6 inches square (15.2 cm). Lightly spray the sections with oil so that the gel will be easy to pull off.

2   For each color, in a pan placed over low heat, melt enough gel to fill one of the foil sections, heating the gel to the highest temperature recommended by the manufacturer. Use the thermometer to make sure the gel doesn't get too hot. Gradually

add a few chips or drops of dye, and stir gently with the metal spoon, until you get the color you want.

To make the sushi rice:
Melt 2 cups (.48 L) of clear gel, and add 1 teaspoon of iridescent gel glitter. Pour a 1-inch-thick (2.5 cm) layer into one of the foil trays.

To make the sake (salmon) and ikura (salmon eggs):
Melt 1 cup (.24 L) of clear gel, and add pink dye and a pinch of iridescent gel glitter. Pour a $^1/_4$ inch-thick (6 mm) layer into another foil tray.

To make the wasabi sauce (Japanese horseradish mustard sauce):
Melt $^1/_2$ cup (.12 L) of clear gel, and add fluorescent green dye and $^1/_4$ teaspoon of iridescent gel glitter. Pour a $^1/_4$-inch-thick (6 mm) layer into the third foil tray.

To make the nori (seaweed):
Melt 1 cup (.24 L) of clear gel, and add very dark green dye (or mixed green and brown dye). Do not add glitter. Pour a $^1/_4$-inch-thick (6 mm) layer into the last foil tray.

3   When all four layers are completely cool, use the pizza cutter to slice them into strips and shapes, using the photograph and the following dimensions as a guide. Use a sharp knife to dice and chop the gel.

To make the rectangles of nigiri-zushi:
Cut a $2^1/_2 \times 1^1/_2$-inch (6.4 × 3.2 cm) rectangular block of the white gel. Cut a $3^1/_2 \times ^3/_4$-inch (8.9 × 1.9 cm) slice of the pink gel. Cut the edges of the pink gel on a diagonal and place it on top of the white gel. Repeat this process to make the second piece of salmon sushi.

To make the oshi-zushi squares:

Cut off a 1½-inch (3.8 cm) square of the remaining white gel. Slice off about 1 tablespoon of the pink gel and chop or dice it into tiny chunks, to simulate the look of fish eggs. Place the chunks on top of the white gel square. Repeat the process to make the second piece.

the lengths listed here. Pink: ⅜ inch (9.5 mm); fluorescent green: 1½ inches (3.8 cm); white: 3 inches (7.6 cm); and dark green: 5 inches (12.7 cm).

Working from the inside out, roll the layers of gel just as you would roll a carpet, holding the layers gently with your fingers and thumbs of both hands. Lay the tiny pink rectangles on the edge of the light green rectangle and roll them, then lay them on the white rectangle and roll again. Finally wrap all three layers in the dark green layer. Lightly press the end of the "seaweed"—it will adhere to itself and keep the wrap tight. Repeat the process to make the second roll.

4   *To make the soy sauce:*
Melt about 2 tablespoons of gel (see step 2), and add dark brown dye. Pour the tinted gel into a small "soy sauce dish."

5   Store the colored gel between layers of wax paper in the refrigerator until ready for use. The colors of the gel will bleed into one another if they are kept together for too long.

6   Arrange all the pieces and insert short wicks in the ones you'd like to use as candles.

To make the wasabi sauce:
Slice off about 1 tablespoon of the fluorescent green gel, chop or dice it into tiny chunks, and arrange them on the serving plate.

To make the maki-zushi rolls:
Slice each of the four colors into 1¼-inch-wide (6 mm) strips. Then cut a rectangle from each strip, in

Design Tips

Try your hand at making other multicolored, slice-and-roll candle display projects to resemble fun things such as pastries with colored jelly layers, ice-cream cake rolls, flowers, candy canes, braided ropes—the ideas could roll on forever.

Whiskey Sour Cocktail

This clever candle is a perfect decoration for your next cocktail party!

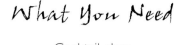

Designer
TERRY TAYLOR

What You Need

Cocktail glass

Pan

Clip-on pan thermometer

Candle gel wax

Gel candle dye: brown, red, and yellow

Double boiler

Knife

White paraffin wax

Wick

Glass cherry

Instructions

1 In a pan placed over low heat, melt enough gel to fill the glass, heating the gel to the highest temperature recommended by the manufacturer. Use the thermometer to make sure the gel doesn't get too hot.

2 To get the amber color: for every 3 drops (or chips) of brown, add 1 part red, and 1½ parts yellow. To test the color, pour a small amount in a glass, or put a few drops on heavy white paper.

3 Pour gel to 1 inch (2.5 cm) below the rim.

4 With the knife, cut three or four ice-cube-shaped rectangles of white paraffin wax and place them in the gel when it has cooled slightly. Insert the wick and the glass cherry.

Design Tip
Don't try to use real cherries—
they don't last and they can turn the gel murky.

Tri-Color Garden Torches

The angled layers of these outdoor garden party torches look stunning, whether sunlight is filtering through them during the late afternoon, or candle light is dancing on their tops at night.

What You Need

Clip-on pan thermometer

Pan

Clear glass containers

Candle gel wax

Gel dye in red, green and gold

Wicks

Dish rack

Dish towels

Designer
ALLISON SMITH

Instructions

1   Set the glass containers in a dish rack, tilting each one at an angle. Pad dish towels around each one to prop it up so that it won't shift.

2   In a pan placed over low heat, melt enough gel to fill one layer in both the containers, heating the gel to the highest temperature recommended by the manufacturer. Use the thermometer to make sure the gel doesn't get too hot. Gradually add a few chips or drops of dye until you get the intense color you want.

3   Pour the gel into both containers. Let the gel cool completely. The towels will help reduce bubbling by slowing down the cooling process.

4   Reposition the containers at the opposite angle, then repeat steps 1 to 3 at the opposite angle, using the second color.

5   When the second layers are completely cooled, reposition the containers upright, so the final layers are level. Repeat steps 1 to 3.

6   When the top layers are almost cool, insert the wicks.

Design Tip
Outdoor candles can attract bugs. Spoon out any bugs that get trapped in the gel and smooth the top of the gel with the flame from a butane barbecue lighter.

Pink Party Roses

Designers
ALLISON SMITH and
TERRY TAYLOR

The glistening pink roses and the pretty glass cake stand make a show-stopping centerpiece.

What You Need

Cake stand

Paper

Pencil

Rose flower molds in two sizes

Teardrop or leaf-shaped cookie cutter

Spray oil

Pan (or pans)

Clip-on pan thermometer

Candle gel wax

Gel candle dye, pink and green

Metal spoon

Iridescent gel glitter

Ladle

Cookie sheet

Aluminum foil

Wicks

Utility knife (optional)

Glass baking dish (optional)

Design Tip

For a spectacular buffet table, make several displays with roses of different colors on a variety of cake stands.

Instructions

1 Sketch out a design for the placement of the roses and their leaves, so you can estimate how many you need. If you want the display to stay lit for a long time, make enough extra candles to replace the roses as needed.

2 The bottom of each rose must be flat so that it will rest firmly on the glass stand. Test fill your mold with water. If it's not level, determine how to prop it up so it is, or find another surface on which to set the mold before you pour in your gel.

3 Spray the molds and the inside of the cookie cutter with oil so the gel will be easy to remove.

4 In a pan placed over low heat, melt enough gel for the rose molds, heating the gel to the highest temperature recommended by the manufacturer. Use the thermometer to make sure the gel doesn't get too hot. Gradually add a few chips of pink dye, stirring with a metal spoon, until you get the color you want.

5 Add a pinch of iridescent gel glitter and stir gently.

6 When the temperature of the gel is as high as it should be, use a ladle to pour the gel into the molds.

7   Let the roses cool completely, then carefully pop them out of the molds and set them aside on a cool, flat, non-porous surface, such as a glass baking dish. (If your mold has leaf shapes on it, cut the gel leaf shapes off with a utility knife after the gel has cooled.) Keep the roses in the refrigerator until you're ready to arrange them. If left on the green leaves too long, the pink gel will absorb some of the green dye on the leaves.

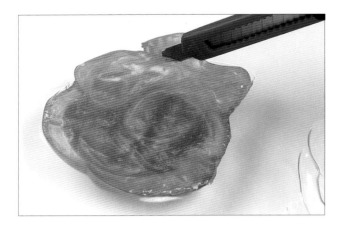

8   Cover the cookie sheet with a piece of aluminum foil, putting the shiny side face up. Lightly spray it with oil so the gel will be easy to pull off.

9   In a pan placed over low heat, melt enough gel to make a $1/4$-inch-thick (6 mm) sheet of gel. Using the same dying technique in step 4, dye the gel a light emerald green. Pour the gel carefully onto the cookie sheet.

10   When the gel has cooled completely, use a teardrop or leaf-shaped cookie cutter to cut out leaf shapes.

11   Arrange the leaves and small roses on the surface of the cake stand. Then arrange the larger roses on top of the leaves.

12   Insert the wicks. Because the roses will melt quickly, you may want to light only a few of them at a time.

Acknowledgments

The more simple a book is planned to be, the more people there are who make that happen: we'd like to thank the following for all their contributions—big and bigger—to this book:

A gel-tower-sized thank-you to all the talented designers whose creativity and willingness to experiment resulted in so many fantastic projects: Terry Taylor, Allison Smith, Corinne Kurzmann, Heather Smith, Theresa Gwynn, Megan Kirby, and Veronika Gunter. Special thanks to art director Celia Naranjo, who took risks and won, and photographer Evan Bracken, who made light our friend. Thank you to Theresa Gwynn, who stepped in where angels feared to tread, even before we begged her. And to Rain Newcomb, who set a precedent for pinch-hitting studio assistance. Thank you to Dawn Cusick, sister editor and gel candle godmother, who gave unstintingly of her advice and her humor. To senior editor Deborah Morgenthal, who grinned even when she couldn't bear it.. To proofreader Chris Rich, who always gives you the right words no matter how many wrong ones you give her. To Rosemary Katz, who helps all of us every day, in more ways than we can count, just by being here. To Jeff Hamilton, whose strong arms carried projects and professionalism at the same time. To cover art director Barbara Zaretsky, who designed a cover we couldn't resist. And to sister editor Katherine Aimone, whose talent is exceeded only by her kindness.

A big thank-you to Yaley Enterprises (www.yaley.com), especially to Tom Yaley Jr., who took care of us as if we were a big customer.

And to Deltcacraft (www.delta.com), especially Jan Pack, for whom time zones were no barrier.

Thanks all!

Contributing Designers

Veronika Alice Gunter is a writer, mountain biker, and traveler. When not pursuing one of those true loves, or remodeling her house, she enjoys working in the editorial department of Lark Books, in Asheville, NC.

Theresa Gwynn is a graphic designer who lives with her kitty in the hills of Flat Rock, NC.

Megan Kirby is a graphic designer who lives in Asheville, NC.

Corinne Kurzmann lives an eclectic life in Asheville, NC, with her husband, Bob, and their 10 children. She is a partner in Earthscapes, a landscape design and construction company, and works on many Lark books as a free-lance designer. She enjoys her life very much.

Allison Smith has a master's degree in counseling and is trained to work with high-risk children. She lives with her husband, three children, four dogs, and one cat in Asheville, NC. She does freelance design on many Lark books, and considers this her true calling.

Heather Smith has enjoyed making traditional paraffin and beeswax candles at home and has welcomed the chance to see what she could do with gel. When she is not crafting or writing for Lark Books, in Asheville, NC, she can be found chasing a nearby river in her kayak or climbing the nearest mountain ridge in search of wildflowers and views.

Terry Taylor is an artist and designer. He's worked at Lark Books in Asheville, NC, for several years in a variety of positions. His job du jour includes conceiving and executing projects for many Lark books, in addition to writing and editing his own books.

Index